Contents

Words printed in **bold letters like these** are explained in the Glossary.

What is a school?

A school is a place where children come to learn and to play. Most primary schools have classrooms, a staffroom, an office for the **headteacher** and a playground where the children can play safely. There might be a school library, a room with computers and a large hall where children eat lunch and have PE.

This playground is a noisy and lively place.
Is it like the playground at your school?

What do we know...?

At school

Heinemann
LIBRARY

Tony Pickford

www.heinemann.co.uk/library
Visit our website to find out more information about Heinemann Library books.

To order:
☎ Phone 44 (0) 1865 888066
🗎 Send a fax to 44 (0) 1865 314091
💻 Visit the Heinemann Bookshop at www.heinemann.co.uk/library to browse our catalogue and order online.

First published in Great Britain by Heinemann Library, Halley Court, Jordan Hill, Oxford OX2 8EJ, a division of Reed Educational and Professional Publishing Ltd. Heinemann is a registered trademark of Reed Educational & Professional Publishing Ltd.

OXFORD MELBOURNE AUCKLAND JOHANNESBURG BLANTYRE
GABORONE IBADAN PORTSMOUTH (NH) USA CHICAGO

Designed by Celia Floyd
Illustrations by Jo Brooker
Originated by Dot Gradations
Printed in Hong Kong/China

ISBN 0 431 15002 8   (hardback)
07 06 05 04 03
10 9 8 7 6 5 4 3 2 1

ISBN 0 431 15008 7   (paperback)
07 06 05 04 03
10 9 8 7 6 5 4 3 2 1

British Library Cataloguing in Publication Data
Pickford, Tony
   What is it like at school?
   1. Schools – Juvenile literature
   I. Title
   371

Acknowledgements
The Publishers would like to thank the following for permission to reproduce photographs:
All Photos by John Walmsley except p8 Environmental Images: Dorothy Burrows.

Cover photograph reproduced with permission of John Walmsley.

Thanks also to the following headteachers: Linda Shatford of Milton Church of England School in Abingdon, Sue Nunnery of Derwentwater Primary School in Acton, Ann Parham of St Peter's Church of England School in Bampton and Irene Smith of Pyrford Church of England School in Woking.

Every effort has been made to contact copyright holders of any material reproduced in this book. Any omissions will be rectified in subsequent printings if notice is given to the Publisher.

Schools are not all the same. Some primary schools have children from five to eleven years old. Others might have a **nursery** for even younger children.

In some places, there are large schools with many classrooms and lots of teachers. In other places, schools may have only a few classes and a small number of teachers.

These children are enjoying eating packed lunches in their school's hall.

What size is your school?

Schools can be large or small, old or new. How many children come to your school? You could find out by asking your teacher. We can measure the size of a school by counting the number of children that go there. Or we can measure the size of the school building and the amount of land that surrounds it.

This school is big because it has many pupils and teachers.

The school in the picture on page 6 is near the middle of a large town. The building is quite old and there are classrooms on three floors.

The school in the picture below is a **modern** building. It was built at the same time as the large **estate** of houses which surround it.

This is a big school too because there is plenty of land around the school buildings.

Small schools

Smaller schools can often be found in villages. The school in the picture is a **modern** building, but it only has a few classrooms and a small hall. Lots of new houses have been built near to the school and now the building is too small for the number of children who want to come to it.

This school is a modern building. It even has a climbing area in the playground.

This school is in a small village in the countryside. Is this like your school?

Is your school a small school? It might be small because it was built many years ago when there were not many families living in the area. Small schools are friendly places where everyone can get to know each other.

What is it made of?

Look at your school building. What **building materials** can you see? You might see walls of stone, brick or **concrete**. Window **frames** might be made out of wood, metal or plastic.

Sometimes schools are built of stone. The roof will be made of flat, grey slabs called slate. Not many new schools are built of stone, so if your school is built of stone it is likely to be old.

This older school building has brick walls, wooden window frames and a roof made of slates.

Many schools are built using bricks. Bricks are smaller and smoother than building stones with even, **oblong** sides. They are made from clay, sand and other materials in **factories**. Bricks will often be a reddish colour.

Sometimes other building materials are used. In some places schools are built out of large, flat concrete blocks.

Plastic, wood and concrete, as well as bricks, have been used to build this modern school.

Outside a school

If your school is near a main road then **traffic** will pass by every day. Many schools have a school crossing patrol to help children to cross the road safely.

The school crossing patrol has to wear a bright yellow, **reflective** waistcoat so that drivers can see him or her.

This school crossing patrol is a dad whose children go to the local primary school.

When children want to cross the road, the crossing patrol looks up and down the road and waits for a gap in the traffic. Then he or she walks into the road and holds up a stop sign. The children must walk across the road sensibly. Do you know why you should walk and not run?

Even if your school is on a quiet street, you will see special markings on the road outside the school. Do you know why they are there?

These markings on the road tell drivers not to park their cars near the school gates.

The playground

Nearly all schools have an area outside where children can play called the playground. It is a noisy place with lots of children talking, laughing and playing games. What games do you play at break-times and lunchtimes? Do boys and girls play together? Can you think of games that everyone can play?

These children are having great fun playing with their ball at playtime.

*This school has interesting markings on the playground. There is a **compass** marked out showing north, south, east and west.*

School playgrounds often have coloured markings which might be used during lessons or at playtimes. Sometimes pitches are marked out for PE lessons. There might be number lines or number snakes for use in lessons on sunny days.

The playing field

Many schools have large grassy areas called playing fields. In the winter, the school football team might play matches against other schools.

In summer, playing fields are often used by children at break-times and lunchtime to play games. Classes will also use the playing field to play games of rounders and to practise their races for the school sports day.

On sports day the playing field has white lines marked out for the races.

These children are enjoying a games lesson on their school's playing field.

After school hours, older children sometimes gather on the playing field and kick a ball about. The playing field may also be used by local people as a place to walk their dogs. Is this a good idea?

Does your school have a playing field? What games do you play on it? Do you play different games in winter and summer?

Wild area

There is sometimes a wild area in the school grounds. Here the grass is allowed to grow longer. Bushes and trees have been planted to attract birds, butterflies and insects.

The children measured out a corner of the field and drew maps to show where they would like the different plants to be placed.

The children care for their school's garden. They plant seeds and pull out weeds.

These children are looking very carefully and drawing the plants that grow around their school.

The children found out that the best plants are those that grow slowly. They do not become overgrown and tangled too quickly.

The wild area is used a lot by children in the school. They draw the plants and flowers. They count how many small creatures, such as woodlice, can be found under stones and pieces of wood. Does your school have a wild area?

In the classroom

In some schools, each class of children will have a separate room where they do all their work. In other schools, there is a large open space split up into smaller class areas by bookshelves and displays. There is often an area where children can do messy activities like painting or playing with sand and water. What is your classroom like?

The children are working hard in this classroom. They are doing different things.

Your classroom will probably have tables and chairs where you can sit and do your work. There might be a corner for the computer, a writing table and a quiet reading corner. Are there any other special places in your classroom?

You could make a plan of your classroom as it is now. You could then try to make another plan showing a way in which the layout could be improved.

A plan of your classroom might look like this.

A classroom display

This classroom display shows some maps of the area around the school that have been drawn by children. The children went for a walk around the area. They had to note down things that they saw. When they got back in the classroom, the children drew maps that would help someone new to the school to find their way around.

These maps are all different and show that maps can be drawn in different ways.

Everyone's map is different – some are like big pictures and some are like real maps which show a **bird's eye view** of the area. The children have drawn the same things in different ways.

It has been decided that next time the children draw a map they will try to use **symbols**. Everyone will then be able to understand each other's maps.

This table display has books about a country that a child has visited. What displays do you have in your classroom?

Special rooms in a school

As well as special places in the classroom, there are also special rooms in a school building. The largest room in most schools is the hall, which is used for school assemblies. Sometimes the hall will be used for other things as well. There might be **apparatus** in the hall for PE lessons and often hot lunches are served in the hall.

When a special visitor comes to school, they can talk to all the classes in the school hall.

Schools also have small rooms in which special jobs are done. The **headteacher** will have an office in which he or she can get on with work in peace and quiet. The school **secretary** might also have an office. She meets visitors when they come to the school.

Many schools now have special rooms in which all the computers are kept. Does your school have a computer room?

Who works there?

Teachers and children are not the only people who work in a school. Every school has a caretaker whose job it is to look after the school building.

There will be cleaners to help keep the school clean and tidy. Next time you do a messy activity in school, remember that you are making extra work for the cleaners.

This school cleaner is polishing the floor with a special machine. Can you see the other cleaning machine in the picture?

Most schools have a kitchen which is used to prepare meals for lunchtime. In some schools there will be a cook and helpers to cook the meals. In other schools, the meals are brought in ready-cooked from another kitchen.

There will be other helpers too. Most schools have a lunchtime **supervisor** who makes sure that children are safe and sensible at lunchtime.

The school cook has to make sure that there are enough meals for all those who want them at lunchtime.

Activities

Try to draw a plan of your school. Remember a plan is a **bird's eye view**. Imagine you are looking down on the school from above and think of all the things that you could see. When you have drawn your plan, you could add labels to describe all the different areas.

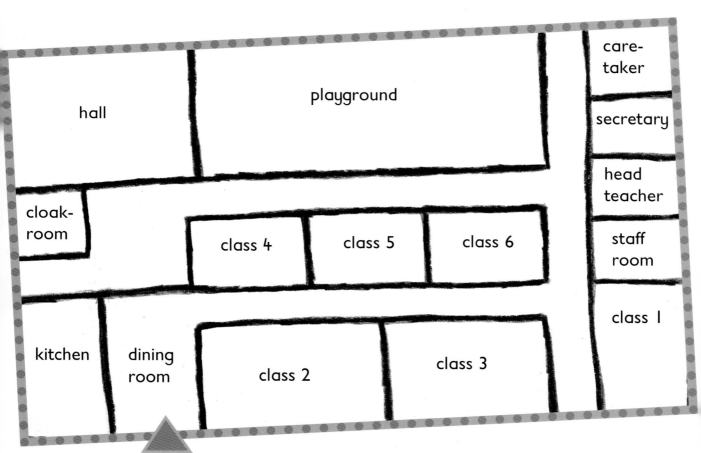

This is what a bird's eye view of your school might look like.

There are lots of activities that go on in different parts of the school. Colour in your plan to show the activities in all the different places. You could use different colours for:

- classrooms
- areas that are shared by different classes, such as the assembly hall
- cloakrooms
- the staffroom and offices
- the kitchen
- areas where children play.

This school plan has similar areas marked in the same colour.

Find out for yourself

Places to visit

There are places that you can visit to find out about schools in the past. If you visit Wigan Pier or Macclesfield Sunday School Museum, you can dress up like a child in school over 100 years ago and find out at first-hand what the lessons were like then.

Websites

If you want to find out about schools in other places, go to www.learningalive.co.uk to find a list of primary school websites.

Books

In your neighbourhood: Schools, Franklin Watts, 2001

What was it like in the past? At school, Louise and Richard Spilsbury, Heinemann Library, 2002

Glossary

apparatus climbing frames, boxes and ropes that are used in PE lessons in schools

bird's eye view what you can see if you look straight down onto a place or an object; the view you see on a map or plan

building materials things that are used to make buildings, such as bricks, stones and concrete

compass a tool that always shows where north is

concrete a mixture of cement, sand and water which dries to make a very hard building material

estate an area where there are many streets of houses

factories buildings where things are made using machines

frame material around the edge of something, which gives it a shape

headteacher a person who is in charge of a school

modern up-to-date

nursery a place where very young children can play and learn

oblong a rectangle shape

reflective a material which reflects light. It can be seen from a long way away because it seems very bright.

secretary someone whose job it is to work with a computer, answer the telephone and run an office

supervisor someone who is in charge of other people in a place of work

symbol something that is used to stand for something else. For example, a 'T' might stand for telephone.

traffic all the cars, lorries and buses that travel along a road

Index